BITCOIN GUIDE:

The cost of a bitcoin went up a week ago, a gigantic surge in esteem that touched base in the midst of Congressional hearings where top U.S. monetary controllers took a shockingly blushing perspective of advanced money. Only 10 months prior, a bitcoin sold for a measly $13.

The spike was enormous news over the globe, from Washington to Tokyo to China, and it cleared out numerous asking themselves: "What the heck is a bitcoin?" It's a decent inquiry - not just for those with small comprehension of the cutting edge monetary framework and how it meets with present day innovation, yet in addition for those saturated with the new web driven economy that has so rapidly changed our reality in the course of the most recent 20 years.

>The spike was huge news over the globe, from Washington to Tokyo to China, and it exited numerous asking themselves: 'What the heck is a bitcoin?'

Bitcoin is a computerized cash, which means it's cash controlled and put away altogether by PCs spread over the web, and this cash is discovering its approach to an ever increasing number of individuals and organizations around the globe. In any case, it's considerably more than that, and numerous individuals - including the most keen of web pioneers and also prepared financial experts - are as yet attempting to deal with its numerous characters.

Considering that, we give you this: a bonehead's manual for bitcoin. What's more, there's no disgrace in perusing. These days, as bitcoin is simply demonstrating what it's able to do, we're all beginners.

Bitcoin isn't only a cash, similar to dollars or euros or yen. It's a method for influencing installments, to like PayPal or the Visa charge card arrange. It gives you a chance to hold cash, however it additionally gives you a chance to spend it and exchange it and move it from place to put, nearly as inexpensively and effectively as you'd send an email.

As the press so regularly calls attention to, Bitcoin gives you a chance to do this without uncovering your personality, a wonder that drove its utilization on The Silk Street, an online commercial center for illicit medications. Be that as it may, in the meantime, it's a framework that works totally in the general visibility. All Bitcoin exchanges are recorded online for anybody to see, loaning a specific straightforwardness to the framework, a straightforwardness that can drive another trust in the economy and subvert the secrecy looked for by those on The Silk Street, which the feds close down a month ago.

Bitcoin is considerably more than a cash benefit for unlawful tasks. It's a rethinking of worldwide fund, something that separates hindrances amongst nations and liberates money from the control of governments. Bitcoin is controlled by open source programming that works as indicated by the laws of science - and by the general population who all things considered administer this product. The product keeps running on a great many machines over the globe, yet it can be changed. It's simply that a larger part of those directing the product must consent to the change.

To put it plainly, Bitcoin is somewhat similar to the web, however for cash.

What does that mean, particularly?

Around five years back, utilizing the nom de plume Nakamoto, a mysterious PC developer or gathering of software engineers assembled the Bitcoin programming framework and discharged it onto the web. This was something that was intended to keep running over an extensive system of machines - called bitcoin excavators - and anybody on earth could work one of these machines.

This conveyed programming seeded the new cash, making few bitcoins. Essentially, bitcoins are simply long advanced locations and equalizations, put away in an online record called the "blockchain." However the framework was additionally outlined so the money would gradually extend, thus that individuals would be urged to work bitcoin diggers and keep the framework itself developing.

At the point when the framework makes new bitcoins it offers them to the excavators. Diggers monitor all the bitcoin exchanges and add them to the blockchain record, and in return, they get the benefit of, sometimes, granting themselves a couple of additional bitcoins. At the present time, 25 bitcoins are paid out to the world's excavators around six times each hour, however that rate changes after some time.

For what reason do these bitcoins have esteem? It's quite straightforward. They've developed into something that many individuals need - like a dollar or a yen or the cowry shells swapped for products on the bank of Africa more than 3,000 years prior - and they're in constrained supply. In spite of the fact that the framework keeps on wrenching out bitcoins, this will stop when it achieves 21 million, which was intended to occur in about the year 2140.

The thought was to make a money whose esteem couldn't be diluted by some focal specialist, similar to the Central bank.

At the point when the framework stops profiting, the estimation of each bitcoin will essentially ascend as request rises - it's what's known as a deflationary cash - however in spite of the fact that the supply of coins will quit extending, it will be still be generally simple to spend. Bitcoins can be broken into minor pieces.

Each bitcoin can be partitioned into one hundred million units, called Satoshis, after the cash's author.

How would you spend bitcoins? Exchange them? Shield individuals from taking them? Bitcoin is a math-based money. That implies that the standards that administer bitcoin's bookkeeping are controlled by cryptography. Essentially, in the event that you claim some bitcoins, you possess a private cryptography key that is related with an address on the web that contains an adjust in the general population record. The address and the private key let you make exchanges.

The web address is something everybody can see. Consider it like an extremely convoluted email address for online installments. Something like this: 1DTAXPKS1Sz7a5hL2Skp8bykwGaEL5JyrZ. In the event that somebody needs to send you bitcoins, they require your address.

>If you possess some bitcoins, what you extremely claim is a private cryptography key that is related with an address on the web

On the off chance that you need to send your bitcoins to another person, you require your address and their address – however you likewise require your private cryptography key. This is a considerably more confused string that you use to approve an installment.

Utilizing the math related with these keys and addresses, the framework's open system of shared PCs - the bitcoin mineworkers - check each exchange that occurs on the system. On the off chance that the math doesn't make any sense, the exchange is rejected.

Crypto frameworks like this do get broke, and the product behind Bitcoin could have defects in it. In any case, now, Bitcoin has been tried pretty completely, and it is by all accounts truly darned secure.

For the normal individuals who utilize this system – the general population who do the purchasing and the offering and the exchanging – overseeing addresses and keys can be somewhat of a problem. However, there are various sorts of projects – called wallets – that monitor these numbers for you. You can introduce a wallet on your PC or your cell phone, or utilize one that sits on a site.

With these wallets, you can undoubtedly send and get bitcoins by means of the net. You can, say, purchase a pizza on a site that is set up to take bitcoin installments. You can give cash to a congregation. You can even pay for plastic surgery. The quantity of online shippers tolerating bitcoins develops with each passing day.

However, you can likewise make exchanges here in reality. That is the thing that a versatile wallet is useful for. The Pink Cow, an eatery in Tokyo, connects to the Bitcoin framework through a tablet PC sitting adjacent to its money enlist. On the off chance that you need to pay for your supper in bitcoins, you hold up your telephone and sweep a QR code - a sort of standardized identification - that flies up on the tablet.

The most effective method to GET A BITCOIN

On the off chance that every one of that bodes well and you wanna give it attempt, the primary thing you do is get a wallet. We like blockchain.info, which offers an application that you can download to your telephone. At that point, once you have a wallet, you require some bitcoins.

In the U.S., the simplest method to purchase and offer bitcoins is by means of a site called Coinbase. For a one percent charge, Coinbase connects to your financial balance and afterward goes about as an intermediary for you, purchasing and offering bitcoins on a trade. Coinbase additionally offers a simple to-utilize wallet. You can likewise make considerably bigger bitcoin buys on huge trades like Mt. Gox or

Bitstamp, yet to exchange on these trades, you have to first send them money utilizing exorbitant and tedious global wire exchanges.

>Ironically, the most ideal approach to keep bitcoin buys unknown is to get together with somebody here in reality and make an exchange.

Truly, you can keep your buys mysterious – or if nothing else for the most part unknown. On the off chance that you utilize an administration like Coin base or Mt. Gox, you'll need to give a financial balance and ID. Be that as it may, different administrations, for example, LocalBitcoins, let you purchase bitcoins without giving individual data.

Amusingly, the most ideal approach to do this is to get together with somebody here in reality and make the exchange individual.

Local Bitcoins will encourage such meetups, where one individual gives money and the other at that point sends bitcoins over the net. Or on the other hand you can go to a normal Bitcoin meetup in your part the world. Since charge card and bank exchanges are reversible and bitcoin exchanges are not, you should be extremely cautious in case you're regularly pitching bitcoins to a person. That is one motivation behind why numerous venders jump at the chance to exchange bitcoins for money.

The old-school method for getting new bitcoins is mining. That implies transforming your PC into a bitcoin excavator, one of those hubs on Bitcoin's shared system. Your machine would run the open source Bitcoin programming.

Some time ago, you could do bitcoin mining on your home PC. In any case, as the cost of bitcoins has shot up, the mining amusement has transformed into somewhat of a space-race - with proficient players, specially crafted equipment, and quickly extending preparing power.

Today, the greater part of the PCs competing for those 25 bitcoins perform 5 quintillion scientific computations for each second.

What is Digital money: 21st-century unicorn – or the cash without bounds?

This presentation clarifies the most critical thing about cryptographic forms of money. After you've perused it, you'll find out about it than most different people.

Today digital currencies (Purchase Crypto) have turned into a worldwide wonder known to the vast majority. While still in some way or another nerdy and not comprehended by the vast majority, banks, governments and numerous organizations know about its significance.

In 2016, you'll experience serious difficulties finding a noteworthy bank, a major bookkeeping firm, a noticeable programming organization or a legislature that did not look into digital currencies, distribute a paper about it or begin a purported blockchain-venture.

thomas-carper-us-representative bitcoin

"Virtual monetary standards, maybe most eminently Bitcoin, have caught the creative ability of a few, struck dread among others, and befuddled the hell out of whatever remains of us." – Thomas Carper, US-Congressperson

In any case, past the clamor and the official statements the lion's share of individuals – even financiers, advisors, researchers, and designers – have an exceptionally constrained information about digital currencies. They regularly neglect to try and comprehend the fundamental ideas.

So we should stroll through the entire story. What are digital forms of money?

Where did cryptographic money begin?

For what reason would it be advisable for you to find out about cryptographic money?

Also, what do you have to think about cryptographic money?

What is cryptographic money and how cryptographic forms of money developed as a side result of computerized money

Barely any individuals know, however digital forms of money rose as a side result of another creation. Satoshi Nakamoto, the obscure designer of Bitcoin, the first and still most essential cryptographic money, never proposed to imagine a cash.

In his declaration of Bitcoin in late 2008, Satoshi said he built up "A Distributed Electronic Money Framework."

His objective was to develop something; numerous individuals neglected to make before advanced money.

Reporting the main arrival of Bitcoin, another electronic money framework that uses a distributed system to counteract twofold spending. It's totally decentralized with no server or focal specialist. — Satoshi Nakamoto, 09 January 2009, declaring Bitcoin on SourceForge.

The absolute most critical piece of Satoshi's development was that he figured out how to manufacture a decentralized advanced money framework. In the nineties, there have been numerous endeavors to make advanced cash, however they all fizzled.

… after over a time of fizzled Trusted Outsider based frameworks (Digicash, and so forth), they consider it to be an acts of futility. I trust they can make the qualification, this is the first occasion when I am aware of that we're attempting a non-trust based framework. – Satoshi Nakamoto in an Email to Dustin Trammell

In the wake of seeing all the brought together endeavors fall flat, Satoshi attempted to fabricate a computerized money framework without a focal element. Like a Distributed system for record sharing.

This choice turned into the introduction of digital money. They are the missing piece Satoshi found to acknowledge computerized money. The motivation behind why is somewhat specialized and complex, yet in the event that you get it, you'll find out about digital currencies than a great many people do. In this way, we should attempt to make it as simple as could reasonably be expected:

To acknowledge computerized money you require an installment coordinate with records, adjusts, and exchange. That is straightforward. One noteworthy issue each installment organize needs to tackle is to keep the purported twofold spending: to keep that one element spends a similar sum twice. More often than not, this is finished by a focal server who keeps record about the parities.

In a decentralized system, you don't have this server. So you require each and every element of the system to carry out this activity. Each associate in the system needs a rundown with all exchanges to check if future exchanges are substantial or an endeavor to twofold spend.

Be that as it may, by what method can these elements keep an agreement about this records?

In the event that the associates of the system differ about just a single, minor adjust, everything is broken. They require an outright accord. Ordinarily, you take, once more, a focal expert to pronounce the right condition of equalizations. Be that as it may, how might you accomplish accord without a focal expert?

No one knew until the point when Satoshi rose all of a sudden. Truth be told, no one trusted it was even conceivable.

Satoshi demonstrated it was. His significant advancement was to accomplish accord without a focal expert. Cryptographic forms of money are a piece of this arrangement – the part that made the arrangement exciting, captivating and helped it to move over the world.

What are CRYPTOCURRENCIES truly?

In the event that you take away all the commotion around digital currencies and diminish it to a straightforward definition, you observe it to be simply restricted passages in a database nobody can change without satisfying particular conditions. This may appear to be common, be that as it may, trust it or not: this is precisely how you can characterize a money.

Take the cash on your financial balance: What is it more than passages in a database that must be changed under particular conditions? You can even take physical coins and notes: What are they else than restricted passages in an open physical database that must be changed on the off chance that you coordinate the condition than you physically claim the coins and notes? Cash is about a confirmed section in some sort of database of records, adjusts, and exchanges.

How diggers make coins and affirm exchanges

We should observe the instrument governing the databases of cryptographic forms of money. A cryptographic money like Bitcoin comprises of a system of companions. Each associate has a record of the total history of all exchanges and along these lines of the adjust of each record.

An exchange is a record that says, "Sway gives X Bitcoin to Alice" and is marked by Bob's private key. It's essential open key cryptography, nothing unique by any stretch of the imagination. After marked, an exchange is communicated in the system, sent from one associate to each other companion. This is essential p2p-innovation. Nothing unique by any means, once more.

What is Blockchain Technology? A well ordered guide than anybody can get it

The exchange is known very quickly by the entire system. Be that as it may, simply after a particular measure of time it gets affirmed.

Affirmation is a basic idea in digital forms of money. You could say that digital forms of money are all in regards to affirmation.

For whatever length of time that an exchange is unverified, it is pending and can be fashioned. At the point when an exchange is affirmed, it is an unchangeable reality. It is not any more forgeable, it can't be turned around, it is a piece of a changeless record of authentic exchanges: of the purported blockchain.

No one but mineworkers can affirm exchanges. This is their activity in a digital money arrange. They take exchanges, stamp them as genuine and spread them in the system. After an exchange is affirmed by a mineworker, each hub needs to add it to its database. It has progressed toward becoming piece of the blockchain.

For this activity, the mineworkers get compensated with a token of the digital money, for instance with Bitcoins. Since the mineworker's action is the absolute most essential piece of digital money framework we should remain for a minute and investigate it.

caleb-chen: What is Ethereum

"In the following couple of years, we will see national governments make expansive strides towards founding a cashless society where individuals execute utilizing brought together advanced monetary standards. At the same time, the decentralized digital forms of money – that some even view as harder cash – will see expanded use from all divisions." – Caleb Chen London Trust Media

What's going on with diggers?

Primarily everyone can be a digger. Since a decentralized system has no expert to appoint this undertaking, a cryptographic money needs some sort of component to keep one decision party from mishandling it. Envision somebody makes a great many associates and spreads manufactured exchanges. The framework would break instantly.

In this way, Satoshi set the decide that the diggers need to contribute some work of their PCs to fit the bill for this errand. Actually, they need to discover a hash – a result of a cryptographic capacity – that interfaces the new piece with its antecedent. This is known as the Proof-of-Work. In Bitcoin, it depends on the SHA 256 Hash calculation.

What is Cryptocurrency

You don't have to comprehend insights about SHA 256. It's just critical you realize that it can be the premise of a cryptologic astound the excavators contend to explain. In the wake of finding an answer, an excavator can manufacture a square and add it to the blockchain. As a motivating force, he has the privilege to include an alleged coinbase exchange that gives him a particular number of Bitcoins. This is the best way to make substantial Bitcoins.

Bitcoins must be made if excavators comprehend a cryptographic bewilder. Since the trouble of this astound expands the measure of PC control the entire excavator's contribute, there is just a particular measure of digital currency token that can be made in a given measure of time. This is a piece of the agreement no associate in the system can break.

Progressive properties

All things considered, Bitcoin, as a decentralized system of associates which keep an accord about records and equalizations, is more a cash than the numbers you find in your financial balance. What are these numbers more than sections in a database – a database which can be changed by individuals you don't see and by rules you don't have the foggiest idea?

Eric Vorhees: What is Cryptocurrency

"It is that story of human advancement under which we now have different battles to battle, and I would state in the domain of Bitcoin it is fundamentally the division of cash and state."

– Erik Voorhees, digital money business person

Essentially, digital forms of money are sections about token in decentralized agreement databases. They are called CRYPTOcurrencies in light of the fact that the agreement keeping process is secured by solid cryptography. Digital forms of money are based on cryptography. They are not secured by individuals or by trust, but rather by math. It is more likely that a space rock falls on your home than that a bitcoin address is bargained.

Portraying the properties of digital forms of money we have to isolate amongst value-based and fiscal properties. While most digital forms of money share a typical arrangement of properties, they are not cut in stone.

Value-based properties:

1.) Irreversible: After affirmation, an exchange can't be turned around. By no one. Furthermore, no one means no one. Not you, not your bank, not the leader of the United States, not Satoshi, not your digger. No one. In the event that you send cash, you send it. Period. Nobody can help you, on the off chance that you sent your assets to a con artist or if a programmer stole them from your PC. There is no wellbeing net.

2.) Pseudonymous: Neither exchanges nor accounts are associated with certifiable characters. You get Bitcoins on supposed locations, which are haphazardly appearing chains of around 30 characters. While it is generally conceivable to break down the exchange stream, it isn't really conceivable to interface this present reality personality of clients with those addresses.

3.) Fast and worldwide: Transaction are proliferated almost in a flash in the system and are affirmed in two or three minutes. Since they occur in a worldwide system of PCs they are totally uninterested of your physical area. It doesn't make a difference on the off chance that I send Bitcoin to my neighbor or to somebody on the opposite side of the world.

4.) Secure: Cryptocurrency reserves are secured an open key cryptography framework. Just the proprietor of the private key can send digital money. Solid cryptography and the enchantment of enormous numbers makes it difficult to break this plan. A Bitcoin address is more secure than Fort Knox.

5.) Permissionless: You don't need to request that anyone utilize digital money. It's only a product that everyone can download for nothing. After you introduced it, you can get and send Bitcoins or different digital forms of money. Nobody can anticipate you. There is no watchman.

Cryptographic forms of money: Sunrise of another economy

Generally because of its progressive properties cryptographic forms of money have turned into a win their designer, Satoshi Nakamoto, didn't endeavor to hope for it. While each other endeavor to make a computerized money framework didn't draw in a minimum amount of clients, Bitcoin had something that incited excitement and interest. Once in a while it feels more like religion than innovation.

What is digital currency

Cryptographic forms of money are advanced gold. Sound cash that is secure from political impact. Cash that guarantees to protect and increment its incentive after some time. Cryptographic forms of money are likewise a quick and agreeable methods for installment with an overall degree, and they are private and sufficiently unknown to fill in as a methods for installment for illegal businesses and some other prohibited monetary movement.

Be that as it may, while digital currencies are more utilized for installment, its utilization as a methods for hypothesis and a store of significant worth smaller people the installment perspectives. Digital forms of money brought forth a unimaginably powerful, quickly developing business sector for financial specialists and examiners. Trades like Okcoin, poloniex or shapeshift empowers the exchange of several digital forms of money. Their every day exchange volume surpasses that of significant European stock trades.

In the meantime, the praxis of Introductory Currency Dispersion (ICO), for the most part encouraged by Ethereum's shrewd contracts, offered live to unimaginably fruitful crowdfunding ventures, in which regularly a thought is sufficient to gather a huge number of dollars. On account of "The DAO" it has been in excess of 150 million dollars.

In this rich biological community of coins and token, you encounter outrageous instability. It's regular that a coin picks up 10 percent daily – now and again 100 percent – just to lose the same at the following day. In the event that you are fortunate, your coin's esteem grows up to 1000 percent in maybe a couple weeks.

While Bitcoin stays by a long shot the most popular cryptographic money and most different digital forms of money have zero non-theoretical effect, financial specialists and clients should watch out for a few digital currencies. Here we introduce the most mainstream digital currencies of today.

What is Digital money

Source: coinmarketcap

Bitcoin

The unparalleled, the first and most celebrated digital money. Bitcoin fills in as a computerized highest quality level in the entire digital money industry, is utilized as a worldwide methods for installment and is the accepted cash of digital wrongdoing like darknet markets or ransomware. Following seven years in presence, Bitcoin's cost has expanded from zero to in excess of 650 Dollar, and its exchange volume achieved in excess of 200.000 day by day exchanges.

There isn't considerably more to state: Bitcoin is digging in for the long haul.

Ethereum

The brainchild of youthful crypto-virtuoso Vitalik Buterin has climbed to the second place in the chain of importance of cryptographic forms of money. Other than Bitcoin its blockchain does not just approve an arrangement of records and parities however of alleged states. This implies Ethereum can process exchanges as well as mind boggling contracts and projects.

This adaptability makes Ethereum the ideal instrument for blockchain - application. Be that as it may, it includes some significant downfalls. After the

Hack of the DAO – an Ethereum based savvy contract – the designers chose to complete a hard fork without accord, which brought about the rise of Ethereum Great. Other than this, there are a few clones of Ethereum, and Ethereum itself is a large group of a few Tokens like DigixDAO and Forecast. This makes Ethereum more a group of digital forms of money than a solitary cash.

Swell

Perhaps the less prominent – or most detested – venture in the digital money group is Swell. While Swell has a local digital money – XRP – it is more about a system to process IOUs than the cryptographic money itself. XRP, the money, doesn't fill in as a medium to store and trade esteem, yet more as a token to secure the system against spam.

Swell Labs made each XRP-token, the organization running the Swell system, and is disseminated by them on will. Therefore, Swell is frequently called pre-mined in the group and dissed as no genuine digital currency, and XRP isn't considered as a decent store of significant worth.

Banks, in any case, appear to like Swell. At any rate they embrace the framework with an expanding pace.

Litecoin

Litecoin was one of the principal cryptographic forms of money after Bitcoin and labeled as the silver to the advanced gold bitcoin. Quicker than bitcoin, with a bigger measure of token and another mining calculation, Litecoin was a genuine development, splendidly customized to be the littler sibling of bitcoin. "It encouraged the develop of a few different cryptographic forms of money which utilized its codebase however made it, significantly more, lighter". Illustrations are Dogecoin or Feathercoin.

While Litecoin neglected to locate a genuine utilize case and lost its second place after bitcoin, it is still effectively created and exchanged and is accumulated as a reinforcement if Bitcoin comes up short.

Monero

Monero is the most conspicuous case of the cryptonite calculation. This calculation was created to include the security highlights Bitcoin is missing. On the off chance that you utilize Bitcoin, each exchange is reported in the blockchain and the trail of exchanges can be taken after. With the presentation of an idea called ring-marks, the cryptonite calculation could slice through that trail.

The main usage of cryptonite, Bytecoin, was vigorously premined and along these lines dismissed by the group. Monero was the primary non-premined clone of bytecoin and raised a considerable measure of mindfulness. There are a few different incarnations of cryptonote with their own little upgrades, however none of it did ever accomplish an indistinguishable prevalence from Monero.

Monero's prominence crested in summer 2016 when some darknetmarkets chose to acknowledge it as a money. This brought about an unfaltering increment in the cost, while the genuine use of Monero appears to remain disappointingly little.

Other than those, there are many digital forms of money of a few families. The greater part of them are just endeavors to achieve financial specialists and rapidly profit, however a considerable measure of them guarantee play areas to test developments in digital currency innovation.

What is digital currency

What is the fate of Digital currency?

The market of digital forms of money is quick and wild. Consistently new digital forms of money develop, old kick the bucket, early adopters get rich and financial specialists lose cash. Each digital money accompanies a guarantee, for the most part a real issue to turn the world around. Barely any survive the primary months, and most are pumped and dumped by theorists and live on as zombie coins until the last bagholder loses trust ever to see an arrival on his speculation.

cody-littlewood-and-im-the-originator and-president of-codelitt

"In a long time from now, I trust cryptographic forms of money will pick up authenticity as a convention for business exchanges, micropayments, and overtaking Western Association as the favored settlement device. With respect to exchanges -- you'll see two ways: There will be budgetary organizations which utilize it for it's no expense, about moment capacity to move any measure of cash around, and there will be those that use it for its blockchain innovation. Blockchain innovation furnishes the biggest advantage with trustless reviewing, single wellspring of truth, brilliant contracts, and shading coins."

– Cody Littlewood, and I'm the author and Chief of Codelitt

Markets are messy. However, this doesn't change the way that digital forms of money are digging in for the long haul – and here to change the world. This is as of now happening. Individuals everywhere throughout the world purchase Bitcoin to ensure themselves against the depreciation of their national cash. Generally in Asia, a distinctive market for Bitcoin settlement has risen, and the Bitcoin utilizing darknets of cybercrime are prospering. An ever increasing number of organizations find the energy of Brilliant Contracts or token on Ethereum, the primary true use of blockchain innovations rise.

The upset is as of now happening. Institutional speculators begin to purchase cryptographic forms of money. Banks and governments understand that this innovation can possibly draw their control away. Digital forms of money change the world. Well ordered. You can either remain next to and watch – or you can turn out to be a piece of history really taking shape.

HOW TO MINE Bitcoin AND SET YOUR Cash Ablaze?

At the point when Bitcoin was first presented in 2009, mining the world's first and chief digital currency required minimal in excess of a home PC - and not even a quick one at that. Today the obstruction for passage is far higher in the event that you need to make any sort of benefit doing it. That doesn't mean it's outlandish, however it's not the homebrew business it used to be.

In any case, on the off chance that you need to know how to mine Bitcoin, there are a couple of steps you can take. One includes significantly more hazard and fiscal venture than the other, however the potential prizes are more prominent. So similarly as with regards to purchasing Bitcoin or altcoins, you should know that nothing in the realm of digital currencies is ensured. Any venture could be lost, so ensure you do your perusing before hauling out your Mastercard.

Mining versus venture

Before we talk about how to mine Bitcoins yourself, it's imperative to take note of that in spite of the fact that there is vulnerability in everything cryptographic money related, mining is seemingly the most unstable. Equipment value variances, changes in Bitcoin trouble and even the absence of a certification of a payout toward the finish of all your diligent work, make it a more dangerous venture than purchasing Bitcoins specifically.

It's not possible for anyone to state whether Bitcoins will be worth more tomorrow than they are today, nor would they be able to give you any solid answer with respect to whether you'll get an arrival on your speculation, however purchasing Bitcoin specifically at any rate gives you something for your cash instantly. It's unquestionably worth considering before you go down the mining course.

Technique 1: Cloud mining

Hashflare

Cloud mining is the act of leasing mining equipment (or a segment of their hashing power) and having another person do the digging for you. You are ordinarily 'paid' for your speculation with Bitcoin. In some cases regardless of whether the equipment isn't utilized for mining Bitcoin.

In spite of the fact that there are numerous spoilers of cloud mining, it requires a substantially littler speculation than individual mining. Similarly as with general contributing, it's essential to do your exploration, in light of the fact that there are a great deal of organizations out there which indicate to be the best and even the biggest have their spoilers.

Stage 1: Pick your mining organization

Beginning Mining is apparently the biggest and most trustworthy of the bundle. HashFlare as of late revealed to Advanced Patterns in a meeting that each one of its clients has turned a benefit utilizing its administration. It said however, that if a significant number of them had put resources into Bitcoin at the perfect time they may have profited.

On the off chance that neither of those organizations strikes your favor, CryptoCompare keeps up a rundown of mining organizations with client surveys and evaluations, however know there are a great deal of analysts hoping to shill their referral codes in the remark area.

Stage 2: Pick a mining bundle

When you have picked a cloud mining supplier, you have to pick a mining bundle. That will regularly include picking a specific measure of hashing force and cross-referencing that with the amount you can bear to pay. Normally paying more will give you a superior return, or you'll turn a benefit speedier, yet that is not generally the situation.

Most cloud mining organizations will enable you to choose by giving you a count in view of the present market estimation of Bitcoin, the trouble of Bitcoin mining and cross-referencing that with the hashing power you're leasing. Nonetheless, it's critical to take note of that those numbers can and do change, so it is vital to take a gander at showcase patterns and gauge where Bitcoin might go before picking your agreement. What might be gainful now, may not be if Bitcoin's esteem crashes.

Stage 3: Pick a mining pool

In the wake of picking your agreement, most cloud mining organizations will request that you pick a mining pool. That is the place you pick a worldwide mining group to join. It's a strategy for expanding the shot of gaining Bitcoin through mining and it's a standard practice in cloud and individual mining. There are upsides and downsides of various pools that go past the extent of this article, yet joining a built up and turned out to be your most solid option.

Once you've finished that progression your cloud mining can start and inside a couple of days or weeks you should begin to see your cloud mining account start to load with Bitcoin. Pulling back it and placing it into your very own safe wallet is a decent arrangement when you have a little holding, however some cloud excavators will enable you to reinvest your income for more prominent hashing power.

Be careful with "pre-deal"

Some cloud mining organizations will offer you an agreement on a "pre-deal" premise. That is adequately approaching you to pay forthright for an agreement that won't start for quite a long time or months when new equipment ends up accessible. By and large, it isn't prudent on the grounds that there is no real way to ensure those agreements will be beneficial when they begin and not even a solid sign of when that will happen.

Technique 2: Individual mining

Individual digging for Bitcoin is uncommon today on account of the high cost included. Despite the fact that you can mine elective digital forms of money with purchaser equipment, mining Bitcoins in 2018 requires particular equipment fabricated utilizing application particular coordinated circuit (ASIC) chips outlined particularly to mine. They are not shoddy to purchase or run.

In view of the high costs included, mining Bitcoin yourself is just recommendable on the off chance that you have prepared access to copious and all the more critically, shoddy, power and a capable system association. Before putting resources into any equipment or mining set ups, it is basic you utilize a Bitcoin mining adding machine to check whether you can really turn a benefit with all costs considered.

Stage 1: Pick your equipment

On the off chance that you are never going to budge on mining, you have to get yourself an effective ASIC excavator. The greater part of the advanced choices are manufactured utilizing similar chips, yet they all utilization distinctive power supplies and some are more proficient than others. The most applauded at the season of composing is Bitmain's AntMiner S9, which is right now evaluated at $2,320, yet new requests aren't slated to dispatch out for half a month. Other, more prompt merchants charge a tremendous markup and are probably not going to be taken a toll effective.

Second-hand equipment is additionally an alternative, however remember that mining equipment can wear out rapidly, so there is no certification that your recently procured deal will keep going sufficiently long to turn a benefit for you. You can likewise select more seasoned equipment or the GPU you have on your gaming rig, however once more, there's no assurance to what extent it will last and as Bitcoin mining trouble builds, they may never again have the capacity to work sufficiently quick to procure Bitcoin for you.

Stage 2: Pick a mining pool

When you have your equipment and it's setup, prepared to go, you have to choose whether you need to mine Bitcoin alone or as a component of a pool of aggregate excavators. Doing it independent from anyone else could mean more noteworthy prizes (mining rewards are 12.5 Bitcoin at the present trouble level) however in the event that you get unfortunate or don't have much hashing power, you could dig for a considerable length of time or even a very long time without procuring a solitary Bitcoin. Being a piece of a pool implies more standard, littler prizes in view of the amount you contribute. You'll additionally need to pay a charge of your profit to be a piece of the system.

Picking a mining pool goes past the extent of this article, yet get the job done to state there are advisers for the best ones out there. More or less, joining a built up, low-expense pool is probably going to be your most logical option, however you may have particular needs which just some will take into account.

Stage 3: Download the correct programming

The last strides to beginning to mine Bitcoins include downloading the correct programming and connecting up your equipment with a protected wallet. There are group of various alternatives, yet they all basically a similar thing. The real setup procedure of your picked equipment and programming will be subject to your decisions up to this point, yet in the event that you've done everything accurately, you ought to be prepared to mine. Interface your mineworker up to your PC, login to your pool, begin the product and you're mining.

Stage 4: Check the numbers

From here, the most critical thing you can do is remain side by side of the numbers included. As Bitcoin trouble goes up, you have to ensure your set up is remaining gainful. Is it true that you are procuring enough Bitcoins to take care of your power costs? Are your Bitcoin digger's temperatures remaining sufficiently low that they wouldn't wear out? Is your framework remaining sufficiently calm to not bother your neighbors?

On the off chance that you addressed yes to those, at that point kick back and watch your Bitcoins heap up. Or on the other hand offer them. Or then again change over them into something different. It's thoroughly up to you.

So how might you be a piece of the activity?

Putting resources into Bitcoin for the Regular person.

The least complex way the Regular person can put resources into Bitcoin is to inside and out get a few. Purchasing BTC today is less complex than any time in recent memory, with numerous set up firms in the US and abroad associated with the matter of purchasing and offering bitcoins. For financial specialists in the USA, the least difficult arrangement is Coinbase. The organization pitches BTC to clients at an increase that is as a rule around 1% over the present market cost.

For Americans, Coinbase has a choice to connect your financial balance to your Coinbase wallet. This makes future installment exchanges simpler. The organization additionally offers programmed bitcoin purchasing at customary interims. For instance, say you need to purchase $50 in bitcoins each first or second of the month, directly after you get your paycheck. You would setup be able to an auto-purchase for that sum on Coinbase. Consider a couple of provisos before you begin utilizing this administration. On the off chance that you issue a programmed purchase arrange, you won't have control over the cost at which the BTC is purchased. Next thing to note is that Coinbase isn't a bitcoin trade, you are purchasing/offering your coins specifically from the firm, which thus needs to source them from different purchasers. This makes issues or postpones when executing orders amid quick market moves.

For brokers that need a customary bitcoin trade, BitStamp might be a superior choice. With BitStamp, you are exchanging with different clients and not the organization, which just goes about as a go between. Liquidity is higher and you can quite often discover someone else to take the opposite side of your exchange. The expenses begin at 0.5% and go the distance down to 0.2% on the off chance that you have exchanged over $150,000 in the previous 30 days.

Different Approaches to Purchase Bitcoins

Trades are by all account not the only way you can obtain bitcoins. A well known course to buy BTC disconnected is with Neighborhood Bitcoins. The site combines up potential purchasers and merchants. When purchasing BTC, the bitcoins are secured from the vender in the escrow. The dealer can just discharge them to purchasers (if there should be an occurrence of an issue, document a question following 24 hours). When purchasing bitcoins disconnected, you should avoid potential risk as you would when meeting an outsider. Meet amid the daytime at an open place and if conceivable, bring a companion.

Now you know how to purchase Bitcoins, however do you know what you're really purchasing? Investopedia Foundation's course Digital currency for Novices gives an intensive clarification of the universe of crypto, from blockchain nuts and bolts to demystifying altcoins. What's more, for just $99, it's an extraordinary method to get your foot in the entryway with digital currency. Look at it today!]

The primary concern

Bitcoin is hot right now and financial specialists and investment firms are wagering that it is setting down deep roots. For the normal individual, various courses exist to get into contributing and purchasing Bitcoin. In the U.S., the most well known roads are CoinBase, Bitstamp and Nearby Bitcoins. Each have their focal points and weaknesses, so do your examination to locate the best fit for you.

It is safe to say that you are a business considering including bitcoin as an installment choice?

This data is expected for enlightening purposes as it were. Putting resources into digital forms of money is exceedingly theoretical. The estimation of Bitcoin and other virtual monetary standards can go up or down generously. Continuously counsel with a qualified proficient before settling on any venture choices.

The Easy Way To Measure Bitcoin's Fair Market Value:

How would you decide the equitable estimation of a cash that has acknowledged quicker than the offers of even the most sultry innovation stocks? This inquiry has dumbfounded financial specialists and experts for a considerable length of time with regards to Bitcoin. While the strategies for esteeming computerized monetary forms are somewhat clear, the suppositions that underlie contending valuations change generally. Try not to depend on Money Road examiners to think for you. Rather, consider this structure and think of your own equitable esteem gauges for bitcoin.

Bitcoin has esteem since individuals think it has esteem.

Your first inquiry may be to ask whether Bitcoin has any esteem at all. All things considered, numerous bitcoin cynics have thumped the virtual money for its absence of "characteristic esteem", including world-class financial specialists like Berkshire Hathaway Inc's. (NYSE:BRK.B) Warren Buffett (who called Bitcoin a "delusion") and J.P.

Morgan Pursue and Co's. (NYSE:JPM) Jamie Dimon, and revered market analysts like previous Central bank Executive Alan Greenspan and Nobel laureate Paul Krugman ("Bitcoin is abhorrent"). In spite of this armed force of cynics and a bunch of awful news for the business so far in 2014, Bitcoin still keeps on exchanging for products more than it completed one year back. The Winklevoss twins obviously oppose this idea. See Investopedia's meeting with Tyler Winklevoss.)

By what means would this be able to be?

Simply, Bitcoins have esteem in light of the fact

that a little, yet developing gathering of individuals trust that the basic Bitcoin innovation has esteem. Later on, the Bitcoin innovation might be utilized for a wide cluster of budgetary administrations applications from installments, to contracts, to appropriated trades. Since Bitcoins are the rare cash units which are required to control these applications, they are significant. Dissimilar to fiat monetary standards whose cash supplies might be swelled by national banks, there are a limited number of Bitcoins that will ever be discharged into course, making the money a prevalent store of significant worth versus other universal stores. In spite of the fact that Bitcoin isn't legitimate delicate upheld by a specific government, the money's esteem is bolstered by the people and traders who intentionally acknowledge Bitcoin for their merchandise and enterprises.

On the off chance that we can concur that Bitcoins

have a constructive expected esteem (on the grounds that in any event a few people trust the fundamental innovation can possibly be progressive), we can begin to make our own evaluations about its present reasonable esteem.

Bitcoin's esteem relies upon "value-based" and "reservation" request.

Note that the aggregate market estimation of a money, its "financial base", is driven by two things, value-based request and reservation request. We can think about Bitcoin's normal every day "skim" as the simple of our economy's

M1 cash supply - the money expected to fulfill value-based interest for merchandise and enterprises. So also, we can think about the Bitcoins which are "accumulated" by theoretical financial specialists as the cash expected to fulfill reservation interest for secure long haul investment funds.

Consolidated, Bitcoin's buoy and holds involve its aggregate fiscal base, which is like our economy's M2 cash supply (M1+money in investment funds stores, currency markets, and so on).

So the fiscal construct depends with respect to the two buyers and financial specialists who trust that the Bitcoin innovation self control a specific volume of monetary trade today and later on. Theoretical financial specialists specifically have demonstrated an unprecedented readiness to purchase BTC, prompting a significantly bigger money related base than would somehow or another be normal for a cash with bitcoin's value-based volume.

Furthermore, that is alright! For whatever length of time that the value-based interest for Bitcoin keeps on developing exponentially in the coming years, the harmony between Bitcoin's buoy and its aggregate money related base will probably mirror that of other worldwide monetary standards. (To figure out how Bitcoin goes into flow, read, "What is Bitcoin Mining?")

Bitcoin's potential financial base is one key information we requirement for our valuation.

Since there is no genuine contrast between a BTC held for trade and a BTC held for venture, it ought to be certain that we extremely just think about Bitcoin's aggregate fiscal base with regards to valuation.

Hypothetically, the honest estimation of one BTC ought to just be the profit of its anticipated future fiscal base and BTC available for use, marked down by an "obstacle rate" a financial specialist would require with a specific end goal to put resources into the theoretical cash.

We should expect that in our hopeful case for Bitcoin, the money related base develops to $1 trillion dollars inside ten years, which would speak to a small amount of the U.S. dollar's aggregate cash supply and about a large portion of the estimation of the worldwide market for gold. We could then separation this money related base by the aggregate number of bitcoins expected available for use by 2024 (because of the known mining plan). With 21 million BTC available for use, we could see a $50,000 bitcoin with a $1 trillion money related base!

In case we're alright with that suspicion, we should simply come down our $50,000 future bitcoin into exhibit dollars.

Bitcoin's "obstacle rate" is the other key info we

requirement for our valuation.

Here's the place things get dubious: what is a suitable markdown rate to use for bitcoin, a theoretical money that will never create money streams?

We have to make certain suspicions about the rate of return required to make up for the dangers related with holding Bitcoin. We should expect that we regularly require a 12% profit for value for interests in certain development stocks, yet we trust Bitcoin conveys five times the standard hazard. We would need to apply a 60% rebate rate to our future esteem gauge for Bitcoin.

For encourage delineation, it may likewise look at how as an investor could decide the net present estimation of a venture that he never hopes to produce positive money streams amid his company's speculation period (e.g. a high-development tech organization that reinvests 100% of its profit before it extreme pitches to

Google). Without income, that VC may take a gander at income products to decide the organization's terminal esteem, and afterward rebate that figure by a rate of 40 to 60%.

With Bitcoin, the reasoning is the same. But Bitcoin's terminal esteem is really its future financial base.

Your suppositions have a significant effect.

Imagine a scenario in which we think the fiscal base will reach $2 trillion out of ten years and financial specialists demonstrate willing to make due with yearly returns of

30%. This would influence BTC's reasonable market to esteem $7,250. Then again, on the off chance that we think the money related base will achieve just $500 billion out of ten years and financial specialists just touch Bitcoin when they expect a 80% yearly restore, the reasonable esteem would dive to $70.

The Bottom Line

In case you're a hazard tolerant Bitcoin devotee, the present costs are presumably tempting. In case you're a more moderate doubter, you will probably avoid a benefit class that looks as though it is in a theoretical air pocket. Yet, in any case, you just need to influence two essential presumptions to think of your own reasonable market to an incentive for Bitcoin: its future money related base, and your hazard balanced rate of return. Good fortunes!

Thanks For Reading Please Leave A Review ☺

www.ingramcontent.com/pod-product-compliance
Lightning Source LLC
Chambersburg PA
CBHW071044240526
45471CB00014B/568